In This House of Men

poems by Wayne Lanter

By Wayne Lanter

The Waiting Room (poetry)

Threshing Time: A Tribute to James Hearst
(twenty poems and five interviews)

At Float on the Ohta-Gawa (poetry)

Canonical Hours (poetry)

The Final Days (fiction)

New Century North American Poets
(poetry anthology edited with
Donna Biffar and John Garmon)

A Season of Long Taters (baseball poetry)

In This House of Men (poetry)

In This House of Men

Wayne Lanter

River King Press

River King Press
PO Box 122
Freeburg, Illinois 62243

Some of these poems have appeared in *Anthology: A Collection of Poems from the Edwin Mellen Poetry Press, Following the Plough, New Century North American Poets*, and *River King Poetry Supplement*.

Cover photo by Wayne Lanter
Cover design and typesetting by Donna Biffar

ISBN: 978-0-9650764-2-5

Printed in the United States by Morris Publishing®
3212 East Highway 30
Kearney, NE 68847
1-800-650-7888

For:

Charles Joseph Lanter
1870-1939

Louis George LePere
1871-1943

Willard Francis Lanter
1912-1982

Nathan Carl Lanter
1971-

Joshua Lanter
1972-

Max Henry Lanter
2008-

Contents

On the River

Picking Up the Pieces

In This House of Men

In the Morning

In the Morning

In the morning the Columbia broke up
over Texas leaving a twenty-mile dust cloud.
The rest of the day was without incident,
but as if he knew something had gone wrong,
absent the benefit of television or radio,
the dog barked all night, circling the yard
on his tether, following the dusted path
worn in the grass from his house to the fence
and back. Nothing we could say would assuage
his disquiet. Nothing would ease him.

At the fence he lowered his head
to see through the warped wooden slats
into the faint shadows on the other side.
Clearly, there was something there,
intent upon entering the yard.
Of course this was not the first night,
not the first time for either of us.

I counted his barks, once, twice,
the peculiar hollow and rote repetition,
the diminishing passion, as if he
already knew fierceness and bravado
would do no good. I waited as he paused
to reconsider, to imagine that he
might have gotten it wrong, hoping
this would explain his affliction. It did not.

In the morning he was somber,
almost embarrassed by the night before,
by the barking at what he could not see,
could not get into his head. Occasionally
he turned to the fence, and the sky, yes,
the far, vacant sky, as if it was the problem.

But there was nothing that I could see,
nothing beyond the fence other than a random
dust-devil. Nothing as yet, though several
fence slats moved ever so slightly,
pushed loose and turned in the wind,
as if some great weight had leaned on them.

Shreve Prepares the Way

You see he found this stretch of desert
an ancient Kalispell holy ground crisscrossed
with trails resembling roads no one ever used

some of them headed Hugo's way into the next town
smoky with burning crude and ill-defined
and bombed-out looking like Baghdad or maybe

Washington smoldering from Confederate artillery
all of them at least three hours away by armored
vehicle from wherever you are and being

short of Marines and other hostile types
willing to kill and be killed with an old pick-up
and a claw hammer (he was a carpenter, too)

for weapons he set out nailing up lines of poems
as holy as Jesus or Allah or oil on signs
like so many Burma Shave jingles sure that when

GWB & SH and any number of other deadly misfits
got out his way grinding up the sand with tanks
and mortars and about to go at it over water

this time since there is little oil in Montana as yet
and maybe down on their luck and lonely
they might pause for a moment to think

about all the trouble it took to print the signs
and hammer the stakes into the rocks and sand
and think about who would do such a terrible thing

on a moonlit night leaning into the wind preparing this
just for them and think about the poems
the lines strung out on signs sometimes spread out

a mile or more apart even going ninety miles an hour
since you must get to where you are going or away
from where you have been very quickly insinuating

that man is a creature always lost in some desert or other
and needs consolation and aid, and overcome with
compassion and reason they might drop to their knees,

clasp their hands in grief howling with remorse
and/or joy as if they had been hit by the holy spirit
of a cruise missile named history or humanity

La Habana

We walked the streets among streetwalkers
hidden in shadows of pillared doorways
and though you could not see their eyes
they whispered to you

we had not seen this kind of thing before
we had not seen the old senoras before
high above the street with laced handkerchiefs
waving from wrought iron balconies

silent in the dark weight of their pasts and hair and smiles
although they could not see us clearly
they knew we were only visitors
they knew we would not last

so it did not seem they were waving to us
or that there was anything permanent
in their intentions not even at the far end
of the Malecón across the shark-infested bay

in the imposing walls of de San Carlos
sunlight flaring off the lighthouse
one of those moments before it sets
its orange glow obscuring the brass cannons

the chute used to dump the condemned into the bay
that day even the streetwalkers were careful
for it was not yet dark as they beckoned
curling an index finger downward

as if pulling an empty water glass across the table
the rhythm of castanets and maracas
drifting from open doors of bars
already the narrow sidewalk crowded up

our photos with men in bright shirts
hoping to catch what we had seen
and though it was there from the first moment
we brought out the pictures later

and tried to match them with memory
the fins of the sharks knifing through the bay
the enormous castle still against the gray sea and sky
the balconies as ornate as ever

but there was no one in black lace
no beckoning fingers or hidden eyes
in the shadowed doorways no gaily colored shirts
or songs of celebrants in bars

and we were not there not even as visitors
not seen too clearly in the minds of old senoras
for the quantum leap of sunlight
along the street the long shadows

of ensuing night stretching out
then lying down in peace
committed nothing to memory about us
or about waving handkerchiefs that day

First Hit

You get put into the game late,
say a few years after you wake up
and discover your oldest sister
is not your mother and the other one,
the one you intended to marry
just ran off with her boy friend
and your parents are divorced
and the dog disappeared
to god only knows where.
So there is nothing on the line.
Your team is behind, hopelessly,
you know the story, the age,
say fourteen to nothing, again,
and the pitcher is finishing up,
putting the final touches on a no-hitter.

But this is the beginning,
for both of you. He's in a hurry,
has a date with the best looking girl
in your school, in your class,
and she's in the second row
of the grandstand with three other girls
who do not even know who you are,
so you have nowhere to go but first base.
And that's the easy part.
Now let's say you're a ninety-pound weakling
who's tried the Charles Atlas formula

that didn't work, people are still waiting
to kick sand in your face, but you try
to do what the coach said.
Hands back, watch the ball.
Keep your weight balanced. Hands loose.
And it all comes down to one pitch.

Years later you don't even remember
his name. Not that you should.
He married the girl in the second row
right out of high school, had a couple kids
and got killed in a wreck out on highway 37.
But that's not what sticks in your mind.

What it was all about is muscling up,
a serious cliché, considering your size and weight,
your place in the scheme of things,
and getting the bat around (as you
have been told to do) somehow exciting
fiber and sinew to the exactitude
of eye and hand, and the magic
after countless failures, driving the ball
over the second baseman's head -
running as hard as you have ever run,
knowing there must be safety somewhere,
some small white island of hope,
though you could never plan on salvation -

watching the splendid white miniature planet
of undying astrological optimism,
that perfectly stitched spheroid, lifting,
spinning against the indigo summer sky,
that dying quail, dropping out of its orbit
to fall in front of the out-stretched
reach of the right fielder's enormous glove -
and running as hard as you have ever run . . .

You stand with one foot on the base,
both hands on your knees, that wonderful
white cushion cradling your left foot,
wondering how, and why, and why me,
but not for too long, already,
ready on the next pitch to head
into the noman's land stretched out
between you and the next island.

Dedications

you don't know what might happen
you ain't careful so you throw the ball
hard as you can like you been told to
two years ago when you got to high school
showed up for the team to stay away
from the old man and they said
"what are you?" so you tell them "a catcher"
coach just looked away like maybe
that is not right "how big are you?" he says
"I don't know but nobody's measured me"
those days you can't get it to the mound
except on a bounce or two
and the practice pitchers say
they will throw you in the piss-trough
if you ain't careful so you cranked up
to throw that ball hard as the coach said to
you don't know how many times a day
two three hours catching batting practice
dust and sweat running in your eyes
you can not see even to throw that thing
but hard as you can all spring and summer
and the fall too 'til a year later somebody
gets hurt and you get put in the game
and afterwards now they are saying
"you got to let it up some cause you done
broke the pitcher's thumb on his glove hand"
so you just don't know what might happen

Upon Hearing Bill Stafford's
"Traveling Through the Dark"

"It was sort of like a wind started blowing
in the room. It was chilling." – Donna Biffar

When I opened the window
that April morning to refresh
our small patch of Eden, overgrown
and much too humid for poetry,

there was no way to know
that you'd be there, or that you'd
not be wrapped against the cold,
or how the wind, as Robert says,

". . . off a frozen peak," might catch you.
The breeze at the window that day
could have been benign and playful,
a breath of healing spring lingering

in the sun with no intention or desire
to invade our tangled garden of words.
It could have been a gentle stirring,
satisfied to idle and toy with leaves

left from a previous fall, leaves
light enough to lift and ride
the new air as well placed words
sometimes drift or rise off the page.

At any rate, the wind was there
to buffet the sounds around you
as leaves must have swirled
about Eve that first day, when life

extended its long, supple fingers
to nudge her. And appropriately
you, too, were there, waking,
stirring, though seemingly unprepared

for the aura, which, now I think,
was more akin to that created
by a folk-healer's breath breathed
into the swollen ear of an ailing child,

echoing as the voice of a minor muse
might echo through the inner-sanctum
of the psyche, the words drifting softly
heavenward, though not turning red

like the exhaust in Stafford's taillights,
but instead, a chill warming the night,
advising against our lingering habits
of rolling unborn fawns into the canyon.

At Ninety-Four Andrés Segovia
Plays the Ethical Society

Poised on a nondescript hard-backed chair
at center stage
he cradles a guitar by the neck.

The background pulses with an alabaster glow,
setting them in silhouette, and then
silence,

out of which
when his hands move to the stings
notes rise from accords cut so perfectly

so softly that each melodic vibrato floats,
and for a moment hangs just out of sight.
The light shimmers,

the light dims,
the light brightens,
with a magic lantern aura,

something
we were never meant to hear,
something not meant to be heard.

And it's not just Mozart and Bach or crescendos
to flare bright Castilian dresses with dance.
When someone in the audience coughs,

buffeting the Charme
for a moment,
after quieting the strings of an Aguado adagio,

after ten thousand adagios,
he removes a white handkerchief
gently from his pocket

and places it over his mouth
instructing us how to vitiate whatever affect
an infected human exhalation might pretend.

Cheering the Mime

A flourish, then a fanfare from the orchestra,
an oboe, a bassoon
bruise the silence
of an audience not yet seated
or otherwise prepared for something strenuous as this.
Immediately, in a circle of light, that is really elliptical,
he appears, stage left,
a Buster Keaton flat-face chalk-white,
long without expression,
and for a somber occasion a tattered tux,
a red kerchief hung loosely about his throat.
Always his shoes are extra large and flat.

Huddled at the curtain's edge
he bends and with studied deliberation
rolls out a preposterous blue stone
in from some unnamed, unknown distance.
His Rorschach shadow
races away from him across the stage floor
splashing against the retina of a back-drop screen
the light strains with a copycat blot of images.

The stone, the size of a human head,
is moved heavily over the worn floor
requiring that he push at it incessantly.
Arriving finally at center stage,
after a great effort he pauses, leans over,

graciously considering the stone's presence
in his life, admiring it as if he only recently
recognized its gloriousness, and as if, now,
all the world needed to see a preposterous
blue stone the size of a human head.

With great admiration and affection
he works his supple hands over the stone,
fondles it,
if fondling a stone is possible.
Then for a moment all is quieted,
until caught in a sudden surge of what must be affection,
he grasps the stone in both hands
and attempts to lift it.

Once, twice, he pulls at it without success,
this small planet,
this dense and complex world unto itself.
No matter how he tries, it will not rise
off the floor.

He straightens, somewhat,
with one hand remaining on the stone,
and swelled with rapture,
and as if it were a sundial,
circles it in a small but dignified choreography
for large flat shoes.

Then wiggling his fingers for a better grip
he tries again.

This time the stone gives up.
But once it's off the floor his difficulties appear to multiply.
His hands, small and supple, are insufficient for the task.
The stone slips an inch or maybe two,
then threatens altogether to fall.
Struggling against its weight, and time,
he works one knee beneath it.
Perspiring profusely,
his face is as flat and white
and expressionless as ever.

Satisfied with his Sisyphean effort,
his desire to elevate the rock,
with no purpose other than to see if it can be done,
the audience applauds.
He does not seem to hear or see them.
Concentrating on the stone,
holding it belt high,
he adjusts and readjusts his hands,
now sweated and slick.
The stone again begins to slip.

In what may be a last attempt
as it is about to fall
he wraps his arms around the stone
and clutches it to his chest
staggering backward beneath the weight,
catching himself,
one foot set for balance,
unable now even to drop the thing
without harming himself,
ridiculously left with nothing to do
but hold on.

Amused with the folly
of having wanted to hold on in the first place,
as he attempts to extricate himself,
a snicker runs through the audience
now wondering what he might do,
and how he might relieve himself of the burden.

Staggering, exhausted and weakened,
he is pushed backwards, at first, then to the side.

Somewhere off stage a phone rings,
once, twice, then is silent.

The stone as heavy as the stones
must have been in the wolf's belly,
pushes him back and down,
slowly,
until he drops beneath its insistent weight,
falls to the worn floor
the oblique light licking over him
and he is once again one with his shadow,
where metaphor and matter merge,
his chest crushed,
breathing quieted,
a small bubble of blood rising at the corner of his mouth.

Of course, his hands fall open at his sides
and, carried on theatrical currents,
drifting solitarily, almost whimsically upward,
away toward the proscenium,
the helium-filled balloon of life lifts away.

There is silence,
again.

At the Garden Gate

Years later they came back to an old argument,
even now, but especially then. Adam still
trying to cover-up the Eden thing,
sorry he got caught barehanded among so much
and carried away so little, and Eve whining
her silly singsong voice in the trees
like a very bad chorus, saying after all it wasn't
their fault, God had set them up, even though
they named a tanker after her. As yet neither
of them was willing to swear-off the serpent.
After all, the market was bullish. Wheat futures
would have been up a full share, had there
been wheat. Cain, just in from San Quentin,
paced up and down along the gates or sulked
in the shadows, stockpiling sticks and stones,
plotting a corporate takeover. He was still bitter
about losing his inheritance, what was rightfully his,
had devised a scheme to corner the market
on razor wire and steel bars, munitions, cluster bombs.
On the outside, this side of the gate, was always war
and in times of war nobody complained
much about insider trading. That's what the snake said.
Anyway, it aids the struggle against evil.
According to conventional wisdom the wrong people
are born in the desert and whatever made
the great oil deposits, when they disappear,

will, shortly, make them again. It should only
take a year or two to refill the Ogallala aquifer.
You have to move before the market dries up.
Eventually man may not need food and water,
and fresh air, or for that matter, air. So what
if Adam despoils Eden, or just to get by Eve
has to drop her pants for a few dollars?
Or if Cain were to kill Abel? It's good
family business. Anyway, they'll get you
if you ain't got the balls to get them first.

On the Road to Baghdad

In the new morning light the old man
and his donkey departed on the road

to the market in Baghdad. They came
from their village in the night dispatched

by requests and promises of family and
friends to bring back wheat for samoon,

and rice and sugar. He would visit
a mosque there, pray to Allah. A young woman,

whose husband and father were killed
by Saddam Hussein, asked him for a blanket

to protect her from the lonely nights.
The old man smiled and agreed.

He had lost his teeth years ago and seldom
shaved these days. Young women

seldom spoke to him. He departed
in the night heat, the sultry dawn,

because it was cooler than day. And because
they lived in Iraq, in the Kingdom of Evil

and were on the road to Baghdad,
with one shot from a thousand feet,

an American sniper killed the donkey.
The rifle report was muffled and distant

so when the animal stumbled and fell,
the old man turned and stood for a moment

in the full dawn, gazing at the inert form,
as if the animal's lifelessness made

no sense, then eased down onto his knees
and sat by the roadside, stroking its neck

where the bullet had gone in, and wept.
He shook and cried with deep, sorrowful

moans, looking up now and then to survey
the countryside, the few trees and low

buildings, wondering how such a thing
could happen when there was no one

in sight. At last resigned to the absurdity
of the donkey's condition, he sat for a time

trying to understand why Allah had
forsaken him, still thankful he had the animal

for so many years, while speculating
where to get another as patient and kind

as this one. He thought about what
he would tell his family and friends–

especially the woman dreaming
of an old man with a donkey who

would bring her a blanket. Reluctant
to leave the animal, he kept a vigil,

twice rolling and smoking a cigarette
in the next hour. And although

he had not seen anyone and was alone,
because he was there with his donkey

now dead on the road to Baghdad
that morning, the sniper killed him, too.

The Civil Rights Museum

Mulberry Street, Memphis,
America in '68 at the Lorraine Motel,
a step or two from the Promised Land,
Martin King, was killed.
Even today it's a shabby place,
enshrined in dollars as cities mostly are,
of concrete, dingy brick, and little more,
unlike the pastoral and Greek at Graceland.
A tattered wreath marks the balcony.

Below the balcony, as they waited that day,
a bank of storms crossing the South,
a brace of white Cadillacs remain,
those relics of America's capitalist past,
sufficient to whisk a soul on its way.
Today, in their obsolescent loneliness
they appear sadly oversized and awkward.

Across the walk old white-haired men
recline on a grassy knoll,
wearied by miles of journey
they watch the visitors,
as dazed today as they were then.

Inside the motel walls throb with newsreel reruns
of water cannons and dogs and police
chasing demonstrators into the current century.
Plaster-casts sit-in at a lunch-counter,
never to be served. At the end
of a pictured road a burnt-out Greyhound idles
in charred paint, its passengers
long since dispatched or buried.
A sanitation truck prepares to carry away refuse,
if someone can be found to load it.
Assured it will be used again
the ominous portent of a jail cell
imported from Birmingham waits and waits.

Upstairs the bed in 306 remains unmade,
and looking through the bent glass,
whatever else might have been preserved,
the years of weather have washed
the stained concrete walkway clean.

There are no guides here
to lend their voices to the story.
It is all free-hand.
Images and facts speak for themselves.

The how is obvious.
A shot from a tenement across the street
rings in the ears of the afternoon.
Those on the balcony point
to the Northwest,
as if the Evening Star has just taken flight.
Each will claim he was there
at the sacred moment,
as children are inclined to claim
the revered and powerful as their own.

But power does not reside in enshrinement.
There is no salvation beyond the resolve
and blood to purify a height
to which one man might climb
to better view the world,
and the steady, unrelenting elements
that decade after decade
insist upon washing it away.
That's the story.

Reading Poetry

Reading Poetry in a Catatonic Ward

It was simple enough to put a table
at the center of the room, bring in a couple
cases of beer, a carton of Lucky Strikes.

a Rum Crook or two, and to postulate poet
as guru, healer, shaman, therapist,

lifting invocations to the garden of good health
by reading poetry aloud. Beneath
the cloth and mask of drama we would

solicit fortune's beneficence, as Larkin
thought, imitating the self, and do it

twenty-four hours a day, seven days a week,
filling the void, hoping to move the shades
hung on the periphery of that finite room

with its small, high windows and particles
of dust populating random rays of sunlight.

In the beginning poets appeared eagerly
with books and notebooks. Old and beaten
veterans of distant, sad campaigns, and

youngsters, groups of two or three queued-up
and filed in at their appointed time. Some

were clean shaven, clothed in Hickey Freeman
suits, wise and well pressed - others
in ragged Levis, Land's End sandals, courageous

in the disarray of their dissatisfaction, a back-alley
bravado of barroom frays. And for weeks

the room pulsed with sonnets, haiku, villanelles,
free verse, an avalanche of broken lines
and weak rhymes for disparate voices, about

presidents and pardons, Aquinas' inadequacies,
a failure to relocate God – one imagined

depths of canine, or was it Canaan intimacy.
Then, when finished, each departed.
The thoughtful emptied ashtrays and recycled

empties. A few were kind enough to smile.
And just when you were sure they had depleted

their supply of things to say, to read, when
the line at the door dwindled, and you were
certain they had vanished for good, they

reappeared, one at a time, walking slowly
in the late evening light as if pulling a great

weight and slumped into chairs, casting furtive
glances at the clock, counting the pages still to go.
And still no one knew if those posted round

the walls like human tapestries, bound by chemistry
and genes, limbs and minds locked in a vast array

of postures, each heralding a different condition,
no one knew if that black and alabaster troupe
of statues harbored in their strange museum might be

an audience. Still, words rose through banks
of blue-gray smoke to settle in random patterns

on the floor, until long before anyone was ready
to quit, one of whatever you wish to call those
who do not come willingly, one of them moved.

    It could have been Mary Kay, who for
    a decade hovered at the far end of a narrow
    corridor where every word echoed a sexual

assault or insinuation. For years she stood,
hands cupped and wedged between her legs,
providing a frail and fragile chastity belt.

Or H. R. Livingston, the self-acclaimed
financier, divested of children, wife, and

fortune by a slave labor camp in Southeast
Asia. He fashioned a repose from a position
held for two years in a Thai Tiger Cage.

Or John Smith, housepainter, unwitting
assistant to an enraged mother, who one
day in an agitated fit killed her children

with a butcher knife. He stood like Perseus
in waxy flexibility, one arm extended.

Or Susan Hart, in the darlinghood
of adolescence, who at nineteen found the Lord
and adorned her bedroom with a thousand

fifty-two crosses. For ten years she lay
abed unmoved anticipating a nuptial night
with a savior/lover who would not appear.

In the near noon of that day, the sun, the drift
of dust and debris of poems, no one was sure

who moved or why. But some one of them,
taken by the slightest, oblique insight, a dry
emotion stirred to life, lifted a finger and pointed

to a single word hanging in the haze of smoke
at the window. And in another day, another one,

then two, until one by one that circle of frozen,
emaciated limbs reached out. The comatose rose
and approached the gray decaying center.

Therapy

Humpty Dumpty sat on a wall
Humpty Dumpty etc., etc.

By then he was no longer the King's property
      and we were not the King's horses
or men, but we took the job
      anyway, a thankless task,
however you looked at it. Of course we were

up for it, at least in the beginning, arrogant
      with energy, almost giddy. Then, too,
imagine the shock of
      finding him at the foot of the wall,
screaming for help, (Oh, he screamed all right)

bellowing like a bull, outraged with a couple
      of storybook bears wading through
the thick, yellow yoke,
      gold-like nourishing stuff, licking
their paws, smacking their lips. We chased

them off, which wasn't easy, and when they
      were gone, (it may have been that
having routed them we
      were feeling particularly optimistic)
there was a plethora of loose talk. Fabergé,

somebody said, maybe an Easter rising, a latter
            day resurrection of sorts. Clearly there
was cosmos in this. Heady
            stuff. But that's what belief will do.
So we set out to gather up the shards, and

cleaned and labeled and stacked them, for easy
            reference. Then, through the tedium
of days of meetings we
            drafted elaborate, some might say
baroque, designs of psychic states we

thought might work. There was Nirvana
            and Ecstasy. Those days we were
all Utopians. To say
            the least the work was laborious,
day after day going over the same ground

looking for what we might have missed,
            then molding and sculpting him
into some kind of
            presentable form, taking care
to develop proper undulations and

sinuosities – after all, our reputation was
          at stake. We enlisted a phrenologist
to pronounce and
          detail his more prominent
characteristics. It was imperative he

have a history, someone said, and we
          all agreed, a past so terrible
he would never want
          to return to it. So we invented
stories, plausible tales telling him where

he had been, how he had done what he
          did, providing a vague awareness
of catastrophe and
          misfortune and how one should
feel about something like that. This he

found troublesome, to say the least, and
          refused to accept our contrivances.
He called for his mother,
          which was expected and duly
noted, then condemned her and called

her foul names. One afternoon, in the middle
        of a daydream we gave him a new
name. A name with
        selves enough to juggle and manipulate
for any occasion or circumstance. And it

seemed he took heart from this. Sometimes
        he'd laugh and we'd congratulate
ourselves at having done
        so well. It was rewarding
to see him like that, believing he could

be something he had never been. In happier
        moments he recalled his life before
the fall, the bits and
        pieces we had given him to
reconstruct, the foolishness of posturing,

the dizzying pitch off the wall, and the
        good times, when perfect-being
seemed within his
        grasp, when he reached out . . .
But that was about as far as it would go.

When all was said and done, even though
        the membranes were intact,
(we had counted on that)
        the cracks and seams were still
there, the not quite fit of the shattered edges,

the tiny chips that had been ground to dust.
        Oh, most days we could get him
through the morning,
        from breakfast to noon. But
nights were sinister. He'd lapse into

tyrannical ravings, not so much in pain or
        against the darkness, but dismayed
that even in absence,
        light could be a searing presence.
Then, to keep the cracks from coming undone,

we packed him in wet towels. Occasionally
        he passed into quietude, reverie
we thought, folded in
        on himself like a dove. When
he wept, if he'd had hands, we would

have held them. The following day, we would
        begin again, as best we could, to seal
up the anguish, and
        contain the expanding galaxies
of sorrow. You see, it was as if the clock

had struck one and then languished, or maybe
        someone had painted it on stone.
We could hear nothing
        in the works behind the face.
We could not separate the seconds. But

do not judge us too harshly. If you will,
        consider the enormous number
of words and deeds
        needed to tie being together,
the adhesive that hardens and even as

you speak
        sticks to your tongue. What do
you say?
        In the end it wasn't easy to be
        fooled.
        Everything was off center. And
        what was
        missing in him was a thing physicists
        call symmetry.
        That's what the bears had gotten into.

Tragedy

There were mistakes made that day,
the mountain air ominous with clarity,
so clear you could see straight through it
almost to infinity, and the lateness

of the summer, and going to such altitudes
on four-wheel-drive roads, or seven of us
crammed into an open-top Land Rover.
We set out in early afternoon, which

was much too late, already snow blowing
through the trees, not that it mattered,
though there may be a logic that says
we were too eager to get in what we could,

get in what was left of good weather, and so
a bit more careless than we would have been
in early spring. Anyway it was the last trip
up to American Lake we would make

that year, to the top of the mountain,
where even those who cannot see well
can pretend to see all the way to Mexico
or Canada. And we were almost there,

shifting down, prepared to climb the last
small ridge, when someone, it could have
been anyone, a young woman, I think,
stood, maybe for a better view, who knows,

maybe to lift her arms and breath in
the mountain air, and the Rover lurched
shifting the earth, and someone, whoever
it was, toppled from the vehicle, heels

in the air over the back gate. Of course
there were gasps, one shout of shock,
I suppose because no one suspected
death might be there. No one saw him

in the rocks or smelled his breath on the clear air.
But he was there. And I think in the early
winter season he too was caught unawares,
for a moment, just not ready. Then there was

laughter all around, and astonishment that
no one was injured. So if there was tragedy
it is that no one learned a thing from the fall,
which was the better part of the view.

The Other Side

Police spent two hours attempting to subdue a gunman who had barricaded himself inside his house. After firing ten tear gas canisters into the house, police discovered the man standing beside them, shouting "Please come out and give yourself up."

By obvious accounts a matter of displaced
location, two-ways squawking, marksmen low behind
car doors prepared for the eventual, the police

expected to "talk him out." But he was, by then,
no longer there. Not that he had converted or
come in from the cold, simply that he disappeared,

slipped away, skirting the police lines, then
reappeared apparition-like to nonchalantly mingle
in the excitement, hands in pockets, his brief breath

clouding the red and yellow air of cruiser beacons.
At the side of an officer manning a megaphone,
he joined the vigilantes, adding to the chorus

directed at the as-of-yet-unseen occupant,
that shade or shape-shifter, unseen, and as yet
considered armed and dangerous, huddled in

the darkness of the darkened rooms, shouting "come out
and give yourself up." At first the privy of his
position pleased him, the power of his

words rising, then echoing in the hollow rooms,
his voice laced with humor, a bravado of irony.
He pleaded, as only he could, beseeching that

frail and hidden and distraught thing, beseeching
what was left, maybe a footprint in the dust,
a bit of breath, the silhouette of heat that graces

the air for hours after we have gone. Then,
tempered by the frigid air, his voice more modest,
bent with expectation and sincerity, he encouraged

compliance, hands raised, to come out, as in that
aged saga people believe in, maybe the way Christ
exited the sepulcher, hesitant at first, into the moonlight,

checking to be sure the path was clear, or entered,
though the doors were locked, appearing in the midst
of the apostles to amaze them unaware that

that for which they were looking walked among them,
and in dismay, the police cast canisters of gas
into the house. As always in the beginning, and

at the end, the wonder is how he made it
to the other side, what prompted him to enter
his voice again into those desolate, tear filled rooms,

and, in having done so, what conjured specter
gave him comfort, what appetite was whetted, and
what estranged assembly of himself did he find there.

Frost in Washington

Listening to the car radio we could see
the images clearly through the snow,
the wipers pushing white stuff aside
in thin rows, Robert trying to read
in the wind, the pages flapping one
over the other, the sun off the snow,

a poet struggling with aging sight,
reciting finally, "The Gift Outright."
And it was, for a moment. At the end
of Pine Street we turned left onto Grand
listening to Frost, Kennedy's inaugural
address, thinking of a new day.

Not that we were overly critical,
we were not. But we had been reading
Mencken and he had a lot to say
about politicians and presidents. He liked
dead politicians, and presidents somewhat less.
He didn't have much to say about

the others, those days, Martin King,
the kids in Mississippi who would be dead
in a short time. But by then Mencken
was dead, he too was history. So we
listened to the words driving in the wind
and snow and imagined a new day,

not expecting it to snow damned-near
forever, or that we might run out of gas
and have to walk to the nearest bar
to watch the end of the ceremony
on a cheap TV in the corner, the images
barely visible through the snow.

Dallas Struggling

One autumn evening when we were twelve
or so, a dozen of us climbed aboard
Ben Walter's wagon for a hayride down roads

cut through fields of corn and woods
to lead us beyond the slow elaborate
seasons of innocence. A brace of lanterns

graced the wagon rack. A harvest moon hung
on the tree-line to the east. The evening
teemed with intimacy and the fragrances

of new-mown hay. The enchanted narcotic
of budding sex seeped into the private
keep of each small space, as we

collected into knots of two's and three's.
So no one noticed the wagon slow and stop
or heard Ben's and Wib Snider's voices

caress the crisp air with weather talk.
We could not easily imagine what
another might find in such a night,

or see Dallas Sutton, who had worked
for the Sniders the summer before,
climb down and disappear into the dark,

then reappear behind the house at
the door requesting something to slake
his thirst. What we saw finally was

the front door sprung open and heard
the shouting, Mrs. Snider holding Dallas
from behind, and Dallas struggling

to free himself, cursing her, and his fate,
their form silhouetted on the yellow
inner-sanctum glow of the parlor,

into which, when she assented to his
request, he crept, and with guile and
the proverbial cunning of Judas

or Barabbas, dipped his hand into
the petty-cashbox, where she found him,
like all the rest of us, enticed by

the twin demons of covetousness
and opportunity, intent on taking
from the dark of the season what he could.

The Space Heater Unplugged

an old song for Charon

On below-zero days it was always on,
set between the patient's chair and the couch,
an old heater, against the wall like a child's headstone,
gaudy and decorated with plastic flowers and decals.
There was never heat, more a parody of heat,
the tiny coils incapable of warming even themselves.
But it purred, a steady contented hum –
and she would not budge, just stared at the heater
as if it had assaulted her or invaded her privacy
or insulted her by being there. She wanted
it off - she wanted me to turn it off, to acknowledge
her presence but would not ask. I turned my open
hand to her, just the slightest movement to catch
her attention, inviting her to speak. She said,
"If you're cold - are you cold? But if it's on for me . . ."
I held out my open hand to her but she only murmured.
I said, "Of course," since she would not ask,
demanding by inarticulateness,
so I stood and approached the heater
she had made into a matter of concern.
I have a bad knee and had to stand on one foot
and lean toward the wall with one hand
and reach down with the other behind the couch
to unplug it. She gazed out the window
at the cold day, the cold, empty day, embarrassed

with my willingness to comply, and ashamed,
but pleased with having enticed me into revealing
my inadequacies, the poor judgment of the heater,
even for below-zero weather, if she did not want it,
the dilapidated and chilled office in an old building,
to show that I too was imperfect, that I needed her
here, to placate my desire to administer to frail
minds - to appear above others. She was pleased
that I would act undignified, cast myself toward
the outlet to comply with her demands, and sobbed,
not trying to stop, but as she hoped
I might think, uncontrollably, moaning
in strange sentences intended to convey
some human sense the arrogant and
deranged always believe they make.
I had prostrated myself for her, she thought,
bowed before her condescension, so now
she could trust me, she could embrace my art.

But the brown couch was a darker grave,
and I was not her father, dead or otherwise,
not even a symbol of what she imagined
I should be, locked in the shame and horror
of that small time she had so carefully nurtured.
The heater, its soul broken, no longer purred,
its lifeline lying loosely beneath the couch

like the severed umbilical cord of a creature,
a child, a familiar – the obsession with power
in an old, old room having curtailed the pleasure
and whatever warmth there might have been.

Convict's Grade

Had they been twins the differences
would have been the same. A lover's pledge
of fidelity is not easily undone.

Walking a receding road one indifferent
evening he turned to the land of the dead.
After the shock, the anger, the grief,

a brother, his spitting-image replacement
was penciled in. At a distance imprecision
is not easy to comprehend. Even among

the best living is sometimes unclear,
a sympathetic-string echoing,
or a double exposure, out of focus,

whose fidelity memory does not
require, but reaches for, instead, as if
a moving hand in the mist might touch

what has been lost, finding the vague
reminders of profile, voice, a gesture.
Approaching the portrait only confounds

the deception. Images may tell tales
but they do not speak. The blinded light
of space separates the points of paint

enough for the mind to blanch. Hung in
the periphery of what she could not see
or hear, in another kind of fidelity

to the eternal, she slipped between
the quaalude of sight and sound into
differences that can not be undone.

The Couch

We moved it to a friend's apartment
over-stuffed, expensive, a hand-me-down,
something of an heirloom,
a handsome addition to the décor.
We would have preferred to keep it
but leaving the city it's often best
to abandon some things.

On the back porch we tried
most of the afternoon to get it in the door,
imagining triangles, conditions
beyond the rules of geometry
not exactly putting a square peg
in a round hole, or even the other way.

It was an aesthetic along the lines
of Aquinas' integrity, proportion, clarity.
We were sure it would fit.
Despite the effort we ended
like Buñuel's revelers, an after-theatre
cocktail in hand, waiting for the sheep,
or a post-mass procession
at the cathedral door, mystified
with failed passage. "Do not enter."
"None shall pass." Prohibited passage,
we reminded ourselves, though this
was to be an entry, instead of an exegesis.

In the middle of evening when the others
had gone away tired and hungry,
disheartened with the prohibition,
we gave in, at last, to what had
always been there. She said we should
leave it for the junk man with his horse
and cart who traversed the alley
early most mornings calling
"rags and old iron, rags and old iron."

It wasn't something you could put a price on.
In that part of the city the shadows
were always there. The kids up the alley
had broken out the yard lights.
Surrounded by the anonymity
of waiting in darkness
so long we lay down on the couch
we had named "forbidden passage,"
knowing it is not always possible
to carry away what you want.

Counseling the Children

My pose is prayer but yet my head is filled
With the terrifying dissonances of God.
"The Last Hours of Cassiodorus"
Peter Porter

I write this to update you on the tragedy
of Monday. During the evening hours
a student's parent took her own life.

What there was of family is now rent,
a woman dead, a mother gone. Her children
heard the shot. All three of them, like living
in a fairy tale. Someone to blow the house down.

Our condolences go to the bereaved
and their friends. We are concerned
with our students at this difficult time.

They heard the argument and then the shot,
but not the voices all the years before,
the lies that lead to a dissolution of ties.
But what they heard is now of no import.

These kind of things leave scars
we can alleviate or prevent by giving
everyone additional support.

You simply cannot talk them out of this.
They will insist that people die who have lived.
There's nothing to do but huddle down against the wind.
Yes, tell them anger is acceptable. It always is.

> A crisis intervention team came in
> today to help our school family
> get through this time of difficulty.

But there is no family here. And if they're scared,
well, so are we. Tell them it is unfortunate
that humans have to witness such a thing. Assure
them their sense of pain and loss is natural as rain.

> They have specialists who can
> relate to those who will not adjust
> or need additional future support.

And yes, tell them they're at fault, for loving
even the sorry parts of life. But do not tell
them there is tragedy in this. Soft words
will not assuage their grief or dispel fear.

> If anyone feels they need to talk
> about this tragedy, contact our office
> for counseling at this difficult time.

And by the way, in the end, be sure to say how
even good arrangements come apart. So, if you will,
hate yourself, but do not point to or blame those
who tell you that what is will always be rearranged.

Traveling West

for SMC, Sept 2005

At the appointed hour you leave
the sunshine surf of some accidental
exclusive east coast beach,
while calculating the time
to avoid traffic, the over-loaded semis,
the possibility of unkind weather,
and head out for the heartland.

You've made this trip before,
every day since you've been here,
watching the cyclical surf,
weaving through the mountains
a thousand times in your head
with eighteen-wheelers bearing down on you.
Even that is not enough to get it right.

Simply put, there's too much baggage,
too many boxes and sacks
packed with the truck and plunder
of what you are no longer certain.
It's all related to misadventure,
doing time in too many places,
the redundancy of what's been given
and what you've accumulated
in the attrition of hasty and subtle,
and sometimes damaging acquisitions.

So you're weighted down, a new Sisyphus
hauling his stuff across the countryside.
It's all there. The nearly perfectly packaged
memorabilia of scarred inconsistencies,
a good love abandoned or gone bad,
wounded pride and faltering courage,
the death of an un-reconciled parent,
old stuff, painted with wrong beginnings
the less than gracious endings,
and other ego claptrap, stuff
you should have discarded years ago.

You transport it out onto the Interstate
70 or 80 or 90, who knows,
the numbers escalating like the years,
out among the improvised escape ramps
cut into the median by wayward semi's,
insinuate yourself into long lines
of steadier traffic, looking the other way
when a police car appears, as if you're innocent,
hoping the contraband, the psyche
radioactive waste, the controlled substances
you carry will go unnoticed, and you can slip
the stuff across state lines, undetected.

Meanwhile, mile-markers flash by
and dwindle: little, less, nothing, finally
zeroing out at rivers you still have to cross.

You dream of the Rubicon, Jordan, the Ganges.
You get the Ohio, the Wabash instead,
waters that do not cleanse or heal.
At least not today. This is a different kind
of passage where tributaries,
replete with malignant currents,
create disparate states of mind.
Just when relief should be in sight,
the digits on the markers take an absurd leap.

Of course rest stops, huddled in the trees
like therapists' couches, offer no respite.
Unable to get out the kinks, or stand upright
in the litter spilled from rest-area garbage cans,
along with pot-bellied truckers puffing cigarettes,
your eyes strained and red, you squint
into the falling sun, hoping for a better view,
hoping to make it to the flatlands
where the sky is visible for hundreds of miles,
where the darkness of gathering prairie storms
sweeps the land clean and you are no longer
pressed by the surge of waves at your feet,
patient as sharks, or the ticking of the clock
with mangled hands you found
in the sand and put in your bag.

On the River

Faro Bowman on the River

Taken from the
Golconda Gazette, January 31, 1898

Report

January twenty-eighth, the coldest day
of the year. A mile above E-town near noon
Faro Bowman with his wife and children
set out in a skiff to cross the Ohio.

For an hour they rowed and drifted down
among the ice flow. All agree he was familiar
with the river. Those who know claim
Bowman thought to make it to the Kentucky shore.

There he would settle up what he owed
at the Carrsville Saloon and General Store.
But below Hurricane Island misfortune prevailed.
Witnesses report the ordeal. Ice-rafts the size

of keelboats spun the skiff across currents
dragging it into an eddy. They tell Bowman
made a valiant effort to right his course. He lost
an oar and what control he could claim over

the boat, now seized by ice-blocks. Despite
attempts to salvage his craft it tipped into
the river and took on water. All was already lost.
Ice struck the skiff and spun it into a vortex.

In desperation Bowman sought to save his
dear wife and children as some might wish
for the hand of God to lift us from perdition.
In seconds, though still midday by the clock

of heaven, a terrible darkness descended
on them, sealing their fate forever. Their frail
craft, not unlike the one our Savior used to fish
the Sea of Galilee, disappeared from view.

Witness
I saw them first by accident, a hundred miles away
     it could've been. I could've missed them altogether
and wished I had, then heard about it in a day or so,

while trying to remember where I was or what
     I had been doing at the time somebody else
was dying. Four of them, two children and a woman.

Looking across, the river's flat as prairie land and
     what is far away you naturally make larger.
In winter the water's smooth as time itself, slipped

down into its banks as if to sleep. But quiet as it is
     it will not let you forget what you can forget on land,
that permanence is a mere matter of words. And

I am thinking no man with a grain of sense would
        take a family out on a day like this. But Faro
had burned the ground up around him. And river

fishing's not a business, if it ever is, in winter for
        a man with wife and children. He knew this
stretch of water well enough, he'd been on a river

menaced like this with ice before. Out of good fortune
        men sometimes assume more than they should.
Or why cross on a day like this? What had he promised

them or they agreed to? Even as the boat approached
        mid-stream it was not as yet clear he understood
his peril. Kneeling on the hard boards of belief, even

when it was clear the river was in a nasty mood, he
        appeared certain in a moment more he'd bring
the skiff around, escape the plight people create

by accident or oversight. Not the end itself, but
        a mosaic of markers at which the course might have
been altered. Was it a family quarrel? A word or look,

a gesture misread that might incite a temper, a bit
        of braggadocio, a moment's resolve to do some
foolish thing, for spite, perhaps. Perhaps a man

believing too much in his duties? Taking upon
	himself what should be left to God. Or finding
solace from his troubles in an impotent deity.

It was quiet for a time. The children in the bottom
	of the skiff, one holding a doll to her breast,
watching the ice and debris slide by. The other dipped

her hand into the water testing how it might fit
	as a grave, then pulled away in horror.
No one spoke but the creak of oars and locks,

the boards shrunk by weather, carried on sharp
	gusts of wind. The water slapped the hull,
ice scrapped the gunwales, the skiff caught

an eddy that jerked them and dislodged
	an oar from Faro's hand. Slowly he turned
to view the river behind him, as if by sight

he might recover what had been lost. He paused,
	regarding the great expanse of ice and water,
somewhat surprised, I'd suspect, that the river

was as serene as it appeared. It was then
	I knew for certain they were doomed, their
images enlarged a thousand times, and near

enough for me to touch, though they could not
        be touched or even heard. As if the river
had been stirred from some deep sleep to stretch

and yawn, except for the breath of wind in the trees,
        the water lapping, the day was quiet. And they
were stopped and held there, Faro going over

the gunnels as if dismounting a wagon he was
        about to unload, his wife baling with her skirt,
the way women use their garments for tools,

the children in the bottom of the boat, only their
        heads visible, even as they disappeared into
the water, surfacing one at a time, once or twice,

before vanishing. Tomorrow afternoon I'll travel
        to Roseclair and join the search, asking
the river to again give up its dead and be satisfied.

The River
I
And all in this the quiet flow
the great eye of heaven rising
on wooded hills out of morning
mists the fog and dews and gray days
and damp forests of the foothills
before returning to his forest lair

while muskrat mink and beaver
tread the banks tracking the grouse
drinking from rivulets patient
in their wisdom and peaceful
in a reverie comforted by the wide
spring-swollen serpentine artery
this vein of catfish chum and bass
this life-line for garter and water snakes
hydra salamander mussel and snail
gathering the equinoctial deluge
the spring torrents into a broad ribbon
circling the continents a placid bosom
upon which Adam and apple and serpent
infesting this newest Eden Potamoi
and Okeanides giving life to the body
a crossing and passing in fortune and
misfortune the long and quiet consciousness
the eternal mirror of the universe

II

Claiming to be shaman they appear
in the mist of the eastern bend
to administer a benediction to bestow
the sacred in their weak evocation
supposing to uncover a new will in gods
that have ruled for centuries
the Black Robes darken the forest
the spirit a lower passage a quiet path
through rock-ribbed-ridges

tumbling down the foothills
cascading over the Alleghenies
the Allegheny
the Monongahela
joined by the Salt and Green and Kentucky
to plentify aquifers and artisan wells
over and through the undulations and twists
of the golden shine of paradise
mile after miles and years into shallows
and pools where in the soft afternoon
the Shawnee Potameides bath
splashing their soft shoulders
their breasts laughing purifying
their sacred duty preparing themselves
renewing their gifts at the source
their frail bodies caressing the currents
with voices giving a pleasant name
O-yi-o le belle rivière where old women
in the twilight bake bread on camp fires
and tell stories about their childhood
turning in the great cycles
an endless spiral of seasons
moving a moving earth
no longer of the world
from which it is lifted
returning as all do to the black loam
on another day gone

III

Man desires sustenance in woe
his dowsing rods Satan's tools
here a crossing and passing
of ice-flows a railroad of free men
among keelboats and packets
gamblers and highwaymen
crossing the wide quiet currents
beneath the channel miners in the pit
of the number seven vein turn their heads
to the hum and boom of side-wheelers
passing overhead and all that was
meant to be is changed the bear
watching patiently waits and watches
waits for the honey bee to finish
his work before the setting of the sun
before the grouse settles for the night
before the Shawnee wives end their song
before slaves look to Ursa Major
before winter fills the river
before men seeking sustenance
in sacred waters are consume by ice

Faro

For months it seemed one day more might
be enough. But the days no longer mattered

one on one. By late last year the woods were
hunted out and winter fishing never was that good.

Last year the little land we had in grain, as well
as the garden, washed away. I traded off my last

ewe for a sack of rye and wore my welcome out
in town with debts. When kinfolk refuse to turn

a hand for you favors from strangers won't do.
Then promised work is never there. What little

fatback we had left is mostly gone. And so
the days drag on to where you come into

a place that things collect where all your plans
shrivel on the vine and fall at your feet. I wasn't

going to make another week of winter here.
The drinking gourd was high, the bear asleep

in his barrow was not about to wake for me.
Then word came up of hiring at Carrsville.

As sure a sign as ever I did see about what
I should do. Made up my mind. Given the wind

was not too stiff, the river clear to sight, despite
mare's tails and scrolls that filled the sky

for two weeks with no relief, I'd cross the river
Jordon out of Egypt to the land of plenty. I'd

cast my fate upon the waters that baptize and
heal us all. Of course, I'd seen the treachery

of currents, the infidelity of sandbars and snags,
and ice. I saw boats torn apart by giant claws,

the dangers. I have endured a few of them myself.
But with the guiding hand of Providence,

the giant shadow that shrouds our every move,
that shades us from the sun and wind, tells

us the time of day, I was prepared to test
them again. You see a woman should not

be made to endure starvation, and the girls . . .
I'd take the skiff across, a tiny ark transporting

life from hell to fertile land. For bad as any
journey might be, the peril awaiting me another

day, or week, the weakness from hunger, scurvy,
and I'd succumb, unable to work, no friends,

no kin, no strangers fearing God to take me in.
My consolation, the river running swift and deep,

my life marked out so many years by His
almighty plan from that to that, brought to this trial.

In the water murmuring as it does, I hear
His voice, awakened as from a deep sleep

when man most needs Him, and so just
before mid-day we will go as He commands.

J. P. Pritchard

If ever a son-of-a-bitch needed drowning
that was one. His mother should have done
it when he was born and saved us all. Though

I've not heard all he did, seeing those who
have a voice, it must have been plenty. Early
on his kin deserted him. There's not much

to do for a man spends all his time on whiskey
and religion. The children, those godforsaken
young ones, never dressed as young girls should,

or washed and groomed, no one to school them,
left to run wherever they pleased. It is easy
to know what the future they had, had they lived.

No wonder God got shed of him and called them
home, sad though it is the innocent must suffer
with the bad - children condemned by those

who have them. But that's the way of it, the river,
the biggest thing we got around here, waiting like
it was told by God, laying there, a fat snake on

its belly - sliding down from the east like God's
bile, waiting for them to strike upon mischance -
a divine vein, an artery of liquid life, and

if you ain't careful, death, waiting for fools
to believe too much in what they can do.
God allowing us to think we got His support.

That's what the river did. I seen it done before.
Waiting to pay back in spades for all what
he's done, the money he owed, and people

he swindled. And some he hurt. The time
he took offense at Jesse Packard warning him
not to hunt on Packard land. It is not easy

when somebody does evil to forget what they
have done "It's posted, 'Do not trespass,'"
Jesse said. "And that means every misfit

comes up off the river." Bowman took offense
at this and they decided to fight, but agreed
there'd be no weapons. When Bowman was

beat he pulled a knife and sliced up Jesse's arm,
still claiming when they pulled him off
that he had won fair and square, claiming he

would hunt where he damned well pleased.
He built a wall up round hisself sure as if
it had been made of logs. Left with nothing else,

no place to go the river took him in, opened
its arms to cleanse the world of sin, and
will give him back when it's done with him.

The Sun
I
And to all in the somber flow of river
crossing the land serpent-like
I wake each morning Kohkomhthena
old woman the Grand Dame eye
of heaven a bright star as Star Maidens
are bright to world's chasing darkness
across the mountains and valleys
driving Set into the sea to aid the hunter
and warrior or saviors lifting to caress
the fertile hills the light the way
of the green-corn-dance and give sight
to men held captive by their imaginings
by men and earth's reluctance to bear fruit
free men on the quiet banks of a violent

tributary alternately freed and enslaved
in winter abhorring their condition
wishing to exchange it to switch
emplacements crossing the swift currents
to the other side with their women
and children seeking nourishment
as plantations and temperate seasons
nourished slaves smiled upon
by the glowing falcon's bright eye

II

Men praise the day even as they fear
its radiance and having studied
nature's laws and habits play their parts
creatively taking up the mace or plough
to sing songs of celebration or woe
rising at dawn to offer prayers
seeking favor in lifting flesh from
the recalcitrant soil turning the seasons
from birth to toil following
a blinded path of frozen ground
from solstice to equinox and back
circling as all things circle
as the seasons drift one into the other
and curse the light that blesses them
their aubade buoyant on the chilled air
set on the river ice untouched by
the long warm fingers of light
each piece of the flow a note melting
into the medley as it approaches the sea

III

Men fear the night even as they welcome
its close embrace and give themselves
to deep and dreamless sleep
scarred in the their hardships
and struggles misapprehensions
failures made sacred in their folly
wake without hope the river
pulsing through the fertile land
the muskrat sullen in his burrow
above the water-line waiting
for the darkness as snow obscures
his tracks the moon the nocturnal
mirror sheds its clouded robe
the pale eye of night drops
an alabaster glow onto the ice
the water gathering to itself
what the land will give of its holdings
the refuse and waste of leaf and twig
flesh and blood breath and bone

Andrealou Bowman

There is a harshness in men that is not
    to be understood. Not resolute in God
    alone, but hammered nearly in iron,

or if not iron then cut in stone, so persuaded
     of their opinions that nothing much
     if anything of sense may dare affect them.

Faro is not an easy man to love. He is also
     difficult to appreciate. But he is good,
     and God fearing. An he ain't done what

all they say he does. Yet people thinking
     it made him sad, and that, I think, is why
     he got down on his luck and

then turned mean. When Jesse Packard shot
     twice at him in the woods. And it weren't
     Jesse's property to protect.

He had no right to post what people need
     to hunt for food. But long as I known them
     Packards is always been

that way. Looking first for trouble, then
     to blame whoever thinks to contest them.
     Faro never cut nobody

with no knife, least ways not Jesse Packard.
     He had them wounds afore hand.
     I know. That's what I think

caused Faro to drink. First off he sold most
        of it and traded some for food. Then
        there was less to sell.

He lost his boat for a time, though he weren't
        fishing anyway. The fisherman had
        all gone out of him. Presently

he built another boat, but we are going hungry
        nearly, nothing left but fatback and
        some rye he traded for.

The children are terrible thin, crying all the night,
        no kin or friends to lift a hand to see
        us through the winter,

and then some, when fishing would be good
        again. The smallest one sick with ague,
        needing a doctor.

Mrs. Polk done all she can. The last time she
        was here, said she knows of work at
        Carresville for any man

wants it. And it may do us to go there.
        Faro says the woman's right. We should
        pull up stakes and make

a new start. There is times it pays to keep
      watch on the moon. This could be one
      of those. I have hung

a blanket over the window lest his sleep be
      broken by the motion of the stars.
      The moon is not kind.

I have heard two owls in the dark night
      outside our door. Sometimes I know
      the moon is wrong.

If not there's little to be done for it.
      I think it would be best for him to go
      alone. "We will make

it all right here, till you are settled." No,
      he says if we go, it will all be together.
      That's what I mean

by headstrong men. Seldom does he consider
      what I say. So I don't say much. Seeing
      as he does not trust

the Packards, and others as well. So, what can
      you do? This is what marrying means,
      to cling to something when life

sinks down away from you, to cling to what you
know is wrong, even to the end. Even the dog
will not go near the water.

We take what things we can down to the boat.
This is a fierce day, clear as a bell, yet
you cannot see the sun,

wherever it might be. And colder than ever
I remember, the river mostly fast with ice
and troubled. But Faro

says that don't matter, we will make it like we
did before. The girls are sore afraid. They do
not want to go. They are

crying. I cannot quiet them. "It is your duty," I say
one day they will remember back on this,
on what we done. One day.

Picking Up the Pieces

Picking Up the Pieces

He lay in the shade of a small fig grove,
drinking, watching the paretic and lame,
the palsied, the halt advance up the trail.

It had been a pleasant morning, seeing
the people drag and carry the sick,
and dying, in some cases the dead, half

way up the mountain. You know how it is
word goes round. Everyone and his
brother shows up. They emptied the towns

for miles around, a haze of dust rising
in the air along the road, visible
as far as the eye could see. There were two

men with him in late morning. But after
a time one said his back hurt and he was
hungry and was going home. The other

said he had seen things like this before and
there was always food, so he left to join
the crowd. By then the wine was gone. And when

it was over, many of those who had
been there, those who could, stood around talking,
at times waving their arms. The dying cook

fires smoldered and flared, lifting wisps of blue
smoke in the clear mountain air. Images
wavered in the heat the way air sometimes

shimmers above water. Those who could not
walk, who had been carried up the mountain,
were eager to try their legs. They stumbled

and yelled and wept as they fell and toppled.
A blind man, sure his sight would be restored,
shouted obscenities and shook his fist

at a man he collided with but could
not see. Two lepers, left alone, sat on
a stone, staring at their hands, waiting for

fingers to grow. The lamentations and
wailing rolled down the slope sliding away
as slowly as the day, dragging with it

the dead who had not heard commands to rise.
But the wine was gone, as were the men who
had promised to help him, and he had work

to do. A cadre of whores, hung hard at
the edge of things, working the crowd, offering
solace to the anguished and forsaken.

For a time he watched, then began to pick
up the fish heads and spines, the discarded
bread, and place it in baskets. He wished he

had not volunteered. He worked carefully
around those who were left, an old man with
a gnarled foot, a young woman sitting on

the grass, head down, cradling an infant in
her arms. She rocked the baby back and forth,
singing to it in a soft, grieving voice.

The child's skin was white and bloated.
He assumed it had been dead for several
days and tried not to look at them and wished

then the sun would drop a few more degrees,
the shadows lengthen along the glades and
open the soft night sounds. Above all he

wished he had another jar of wine, that
to assuage his distress, beyond all, he
might hear the sweet murmur of a distant god.

One Photo of an Amish Family on Its Way to Prayer

Blacked on assumptions of Pennsylvania
countryside, four of them, a woman

nearest the camera, a man and two boys,
stride toward the picture's edge. A morning

sun, or if an evening service, the last low
of light that day presses at their backs.

The shadows into which they walk are
subtle as medieval specters, attired in

Amish black, the doubled future
of a man and woman makes a nearly

Rorschach splat. The males are dressed
in customary suits and blackjack hats,

the woman, a dress and bonnet. She
peers straight ahead, as if to see

beyond the picture's edge to the end
of light and time. The man, neck bowed

as if to husband a cradle and scythe,
carries instead a child beneath

his arm like a sack of grain. Its right foot
waves behind him openly where the boys

follow in a line two steps apart. One,
seven or so, the other perhaps twelve,

displays an irreverent bright blue sock
beneath a lifted trouser leg. Both face

away across the stubble of machine planted
and picked cornrows, to a Ring of Brodgor

barns and silos. There is very little
of sky or blue horizon here. This is a portrait

of earth, the humans traversing the planet
held in stasis, each traveler with a right

foot lifted in nearly perfect choreography
of accident, a lockstep, about to touch

the ground again, each shadow prepared
to meet its foot in the sanitary way

modern life manages information.
Their images are without dust, no wind,

an absolute silence, headed for a prayer
service, or so the caption says, into

an unforeseen distance, a service the photo
will not record, an action in space

and time, into and out of which they,
the living and, by now, no doubt, some

of the dead, have already passed. Still
they are poised as if waiting for the picture

to decay. There is no original of this,
except a negative, adhering to what is,

rejecting all that comes with the future
becoming past, a reverse of light and

dark, occupying space unseen as hidden
matter. So they will wait without process,

perhaps for someone with another camera
to snap another picture to release them

from the bondage of their stance,
free them from the click of light

etching itself into a new frame,
trading one obsession for another.

The Wedding Guests

The wedding guests were not invited
from the streets as strangers but carried
to the nuptial room by invitations
clichéd scripts of best-wish doggerel
scratched to the face of cheap boards
for political ne'er do wells to grease the skids
to provide homage not so much for friendship
or to advance a sacramental bond
unless proffered to others in attendance
who pat or pound compatriots on the back
drinking and grinning knowing the code the custom
the woman nervous and then nearly frantic
that the swelling troupe might exhaust
the wine available to her uninquiring eye
though there was still plenty
after the reprimand from a more appraising eye
a better judge of what was and was not needed
to instruct the porters to do as told
to fill the large stone-pots with water
(two or three hins each) still only empty by half
the guests applauding their drunkenness
knowing no limits beyond flattery and fawning
familiar with the Roman fondness
for mixing water and wine readily claiming
in the jest of inebriated tasteless mocking
that bridegrooms as saviors and true believers
be it in gift or sacrifice always save the best
watered-down as it might be for last

A Second Coming

As if being sprung whole from adolescence
were not enough, he prayed all his life
for a second coming. It was a fervent,
heart-felt prayer for a land or state-of-mind
where wrongs (and he suspected he suffered
more than his share), might be rectified.
It wasn't a matter of golden streets,
the hazy misty well-being of Christian heaven.
It was not the ecstasy of Nirvana
he longed for, but a readjustment
to the commerce of the soul, where man's
worse transgression might be the beneficent
weave of a peaceful fabric, a warming
cloth for cold and indecisive nights.

And then, one afternoon, it was there,
in the undivided space of a second,
as if planned for a millennium, or longer,
maybe Saul on his way to Damascus,
leveled by a force he didn't see,
the light in his favor, an inattentive driver,
chatting with a friend, at an intersection
broad-sided him. It was a second coming,
the repose he sought washed over with
that superficial gentleness that most often
bandages and hides the wounds of human desire.

He smiles a lot these days but does not pray.
Wrapped in a blanket warming in the sun,
from the window he stares empty-eyed
into the vacant lot across the street where
throughout the afternoon children swing bats
and chase each other round the bases.

Homage to an Anonymous God

Barabbas knew and to his credit
did not relent. The kind of thing
you'd not expect from a thief,
to hold his peace when he might make
some gain of it. Yet, so sincerely was
he imbued with deceit, he could not speak.

Had I a chance, for that, I would forgive
him his transgressions, the taking
of the widow's bread, leaving her destitute
in old age. All those hapless children
he fathered and refused to feed.
And Ramel's goats. That was a shame.
The man worked hard, only to find
his profits vanished, as it were, almost
before his eyes into Barabbas' pockets.
Like so much of life, when Ramel
diverted his attention for just a moment,
what he treasured most disappeared.

Possibly Barabbas did not want to press
his luck and once the exchange was made,
was loath to question the decision
or declare that it had been made in error.
His friends and kin who shouted most
vociferously in the crowd were quickly
scattered and taken to drink, and as he knew,
would be difficult to rally a second time.

You see, some days before he showed up
in the garden, quite by chance,
the chance of luck that feeds on opportunity
thieves are quick to seize, and that night
he witnessed the two of us in prayer.

Before we could speak, or greet him,
when he saw us first, as if a trick had been
played on him, he laughed the silly
little laugh of a child, so alike we did appear,
as individual hands, each the mirror
of its opposite, on two arms hang,
or opposing feet are matched rhythmically
stride for stride, so did one compliment
the other in speech and silence, word and act.
We toyed with it for months, rehearsing,
mimicking and miming until we were
as nearly one as two persons may be.

That night he showed up caging food
and we fed him. I think the charity
of that touched his scarred soul,
and encouraged him to keep his peace.

Not that he could distinguish one of us
from the other, for whatever reasons,
but surmised in his cunning and guile,

when he was brought before the Sanhedrin
that which ever one of us the Romans
had arrested, we, too, might be interested
in misleading the procurator. That Pilate
could be led to mistake one for the other,
pleased Barabbas' perverse bent.
And since there was no way to deceive
and not deceive in a single blow
he fell into a profound dilemma
of who to betray, the Romans or us.

It was enough for the Romans.
Of course, the crime was not theirs,
and Caesar's servants had other things
with which to occupy themselves that day.
In their eagerness for blood, and wanting
to be done with it, they laid aside
all questions and mistook him for me.

Simon Peter knew the difference
and in that grave deportment of his,
came nearly to giving it all away,
until he discerned the lay of that sacrificial land
and so complied with the plan, though
mostly it seemed not a plan at all.

Clearly he was not a God. The Romans
were aware of that, and so were the priests.
Strictly put, this was an entirely human affair.

But he was willing to die, as all men must,
and gave his life to advance what we espoused,
though it found little fare with the Israelites,
or anyone, for that matter.

But that is how Barabbas came to know.

So, within a thieving heart my secret kept
as in a keep of sepulcher where without
anything of identity but my name, my virtual
twin was laid. An orphan, parents and place
of birth unknown, some thought he came from Syria.
I waited out of sight until the Romans
had their way. Then we laid him in the sepulcher
and late at night beneath a full moon shrouded
by the terrible darkness of a deep cloud-cover,
we rolled back the stone (it was a small stone)
and spirited the body away for burial in an
unknown place that was quickly forgotten.

It was easy to confound the skeptics,
twins as we were, one of this world,
the other a mere reflection in the water,
and for me to appear to the apostles,
in his place, as he had taken my place,
and further blur and complicate the dissonance
between the realms of living and dead.

Later, struck with that blazing insight lighting up
his head Paul was brought down. Realizing
the enormity of what we had done he slipped
into a faint and tumbled from his horse.

It is better that I continued on and he, without
a name or talent to move men
by word or example, should be given adulation
by dying silently and that Barabbas,
who could not chose to harm one
without aiding the other, who could not,
though he tried, chose deceit without virtue,
might gain only a short few years of life,
plagued by profitless indecision.

What We Say When We Recite
What We Have Heard

Suppose the defenders of Troy
had not made too much of Poseidon's snakes
and heeded Laocoon's fear about Greeks
and gifts, especially those laying siege
to their walls for ten years,
and further suppose they had
had the where-with-all
to ignore or better yet reject Sinon's
encouragements and prophecies,
and so had gotten on a ladder
or mounted some other temperate device
to look the gift horse in the mouth,
and seeing the heroes inside
decked out for battle,
and knowing what awaited them,
placed faggots at the legs and wheels
and set the whole thing ablaze,
and watched the flaming chunks of guts
and human flesh, the molten drippings
of swords and spearheads drop
harmlessly to the ground.
In days, Odysseus would have turned
his sails for home. In another month,
at least, the ashes cooled, the Trojans
could have repaired their wounded walls.
But what would Homer have said then?
And would we have avoided the romp
of several thousand years of proverbs?

Somehow the Trojans were too easily beguiled.
Maybe battle fatigue had taken their senses,
awash in an illusion of invincibility
and righteousness too willingly they trusted
their pride and readily assumed that after all
the years the Greeks had seen the light,
had given up the fight. Whatever reason,
they embraced the folly that rakes
the best of human enterprise,
especially in times of good fortune.

Even the great Achilles,
wielding his blazing shield,
serviced by Athena's deceit,
and not yet humbled by the fate he knew
awaited him, unworthy of himself
and of the dead, as Homer seems at pains to note,
succumbed to hatred and vengeance,
and to mock the ancient father/king
dragged Hector's body in the dust
around Priam's city.

But what is this curse, anyway?
Is it the small barbaric patch of arrogance
not dipped into the River Styx?
Or was it something worse, something
myths and stories of war seem always to omit?
Could it be the repetitions encased
in genetic markings of history, clichés
printed on the long walls, the recitation
of the abandoned centuries that we echo?

Family Gatherings

The stories were always steeped in runic tones,
not quite myth,
the plodding truths of yeomen's dialogue,
but no more probable than Lazarus,
of cows plucked from rumination
and raised over telephone wires,
the walking-on-water wonder
of a tractor-trailer truck transported
to the other side of a lake,
its wheels creating a transcendental wake
of water and wind, to be set down
in the middle of a field,
the driver in the cab, miraculously, unharmed.
Or a giant stone from the south pasture
uprooted and rolled into the road
as if by plan and left there
almost as a challenge to good sense,
that took twelve men
three days to break up and clear away.

Uncles, fathers, sons, small, lean
and hungry looking men, cousins,
husbands and husbands-to-be,
an occasional bachelor nephew,
an alien brother-in-law,
on some not too well understood holiday
like the Fourth, or Good Friday,
or the Sunday before a Monday Memorial Day

that wasn't Memorial Day at all,
would sit at the open end of the garage,
cradling cans of beer,
smoking cigarettes and pipes.
It was a listing of connections,
but without a core, a vacuum in a funnel,
a family gathering laced up tightly
and held in place as if each had ordained
the genetic order from which it came.
It was a council for the impossible,
as if each had chosen existence
over all the other possibilities,
all agreeing, shaking their heads,
not in opposition to the verities
but simply at the wonder of it.

And because all things are possible
in the vacuum of belief or disbelief,
there was a story about three pieces of straw
driven into a Cottonwood tree like railroad spikes
upon which to hang any number
of theories about how things happen.

At the other end inside the house,
tilted slightly away from the men,
chairs backed to the living room walls
to reinforce the keep, aunts, in their girth
and weight, small Conestoga wagons,

set up for the night, red with the blood
that nourished the moons of their faces,
the pennants of their lace handkerchiefs
waving now and then in the oppressive air,
infants on the floor playing at the center,
holding the earth to its natural spin,
mothers, daughters, and nieces, daughters-in-law,
converse about the somewhat
more believable, but still mystical.
The horror of the farm couple down the road
found bound hand and foot,
shot with their own shotgun.
A baby born missing an arm.
A family curse, star-crossed,
insanity skipping two generations,
the affliction of drink in husbands,
every woman's nemesis.
And practical wisdom, the advisability
of keeping doors locked
or taking Epsom salts and
Carter's Little Liver Pills for cramps.
It was a matter of wedding rings,
lunar cycles, the endless repetitions
of cake walks and birthdays,
of what was passed on circling back
as easy and natural to them as Plato's forms.

But something in what the women said,
the ticking of the large Seth Thomas
on the mantel barely, but always audible
above their circling voices,
there was something in what they said
that the men did not hear.

You always come back to where you are
and you bring yourself back with you.
There's birth and a time to sit down
between that and death, and no matter
how many years apart, all of it in the same room,
and then the world outside is not that different
from the inside, so it doesn't much matter
who rolled away the stone.

The men were still talking about things
that lift off the average, that might make
a straight-line run for open space,
even though it is mostly comforting to find them
settled again on earth, after all.

They spoke of the strange blue light
that lit up the night sky of the northern hemisphere.
Moving the stone (although it didn't much matter
who moved it) was only the beginning,
the first part of the improbability
of getting the door open to get through
to the other side that needs looking into.

Watching Her Die

For JW

We spend the afternoon making small talk,
shopping the supermarket for small things,
snacks, quick fixes for hunger, something brief
to placate exhaustion during long hours
on call. I watch his face as he watches
shoppers, looking for telltale signs of health.

Side by side two obese women in red
spandex crowd in front of us filling their
carts. "That's what I see in clinic," he says,
"everyday. Mostly from the Midwest. It's
what they eat, a lack of self awareness."

And almost as an afterthought, "I have
a patient," he tells me, offering a
haze of symptoms, that beyond the known signs
of an organism's struggle to stay
alive, has little to do with bad habits.
Bipolar, high fever, acidic blood,
platelets clotting into a series of
microscopic log jams at the center
of the torrent. Otherwise her blood thin
enough to leak away at random is
followed by a litany of medical
explanations I do not understand.
"We've tried everything," he says. "Nothing fits."

It's a mystery of connections gone bad,
small things that could add up are shrouded
even to the bright eyes of science,
small things that evade the sight and insight
connections of his inner senses,
my obvious failure to connect his words.

"I'm going to lose her," he says, finally.
The women push off to other
parts of the store. The isle in front of us
is empty all the way down.
"This will be the first," he says.
"And she's only thirty."

But the afternoon is warm and breezy,
the parking lot gorged with busy people
floating on an improbity of soft light
painting the genetic pool
with its inevitable degeneration.

Resigned to insolvency in seeking
salvation, even on a sunny day,
the impossibilities of altering the flow,
to relieve our hunger, even briefly,
I ride home with a somber man who,
since he was nine, has said that all
he wants in life is to help someone.

The next day his brother calls
to pass on to me an anonymous sort
of shared grief, saying,
"he wanted you to know,
the woman he spoke of, died last night."

Charisma is Lethal

sometimes it appears tall whip-thin
and graceful sometimes with names
like Vandenberg or Hollenhaus

to remind us of royalty
especially in priests and military officers
a proper blend of ritual and savoir faire

attached to doctrines of enemies
and heroes waiting for the organ
music to break from a Bach

missa pro defunctis then to stand
and with frail fluttering hands
lift the host and raise parishioners

from the dead of the pews to their feet
to a prolonged silence waiting
for him to speak or sing

military stoicism offers
paternal empathy because
it knows what waits out there that keeps

assignations with the enemy
but gives orders anyway
if it blinks everyone knows it did

the right thing since these are blue-eyed boys
so in the end it is ritual that counts
knowing for sure the next step

by which souls are beguiled
it does not matter that no one
believes in god or that heaven

is an improper dream no matter
what they say we believe them
though we cannot be salvaged

by a timely cross of olive oil
and palm ashes or a Silver Star
and uniforms, prayers and orders

to "fire at will" are only ways
to excuse our desire to lie down
in darkness with the unknown

Mr. McGraw

Most of them came from the ballpark
neighborhood, drawn by the crowd's roar,
yesterday, the day before, by rumor,

what they heard on the street, when they
gathered to play or scheme in the vacant
lots strewn with rubbish of the tenements

they lived in. Others migrated out
of ghettoes on the other side of town
following newspaper reports of men

playing a child's game, but not exactly.
There was no employment to keep them
away, no youth camps, no rec centers,

unless this was one. Beyond the price
of admission nobody had money.
There were no snow-cones, cocaine-cola

or hotdogs. In the spring they came out
of a gray winter of frigid classrooms
heated and smoked-up by coal-fired stoves,

hoping to satisfy the immigrant
imperative to learn figures and count change,
to calculate, to understand "sums"

and make certain they were "nobody's fool."
On hot days they filled the bleachers with dark
woolen shirts and pants, in old world hats,

bunched up in the sun, making and taking
bets on the game, forecasting, calculating
the chances, weighing the wisdom or

folly of strategy. They came to watch
Achilles and Ajax, MacCool and Brendan
rise or lift out of the recesses

beneath the stands, and wonder at the flight
of the ball often guided by Athena's hand
and carried on the breeze toward center

or deep left, until it was snared by
a fielder, as if someone had told him
exactly where it would come down. For nine

innings every afternoon they slipped
into the garden and watched with rapt
attention, maligned opposing players

when they could, enjoined their favorites,
and attempted to decipher the puzzles,
the irregularities of hitting

streaks and slumps, of balls soaring out of the park
into the corrupted world beyond.
They calculated the advantage of a well

placed bunt, the timeliness of a "hit and run,"
enquiring why Mr. McGraw didn't bunt
in the ninth. "What was he thinking?" or

observing "Mr. McGraw don't make silly
mistakes. He had something in mind.
He's gonna send in a pinch-hitter."

"That don't make sense. A right-handed
pinch-hitter in the ninth." "The leftfielder
moved in two steps." "He's guarding the line."

"What'd he see?" "Who's the hitter?" who slaps
a three-two curve to right to end the game,
a right-handed hitter to right, and off

the wall. How do you figure winning a game
on a hit like that? It's what happens when
the pawns and knights have a mind of their own.

Anyway, that's how it's supposed to work.
Tomorrow? It'd be a good idea to keep
a closer watch on what Mr. McGraw's thinking.

Upon Discovering Leonardo Didn't Paint "The Adoration of the Magi"

> "None of the paint we see on the 'Adoration'
> today was put there by Leonardo. God knows
> who did it, but it was not Leonardo."
> Maurizio Seracini as quoted by
> Harf Zimmerman in *The New York Times*.

Assuming Da Vinci didn't plan this,
what significance might be assigned
to the adoration of the magi,
the sketched out journey of magus, sorcerer,
magician, those paint-pots of chicanery
and deception who supposedly
followed their bent astrology westward?
Of course Leonardo sketched it out
on wood, in lampblack, adding the glue and
green-gray mix made over with white lead,
though it appears that in so doing
he was a little short on passion.
Within the year of its inception
he forsook the project, as he did
the monks of San Danoto, much as
the magi had abandoned their realms,
though not entirely. He absconded
to Milan to pursue the twin star-beams
of heresy and hearsay the word
rumor and myth had sketched on the air
over the centuries. We could list them here:

God, wisdom, power, knowledge, money –
easy to believe and accommodate,
enough to set even the reverential
beneath a tree in Eden to doubting.

Leonardo came out of it with clean hands.
Though just barely. Demeaning his art
for patronage, seeking celebrity
and adoration, he attempted to join
the minions of weapons and warfare.

Of course experts are always wrong
about the truth, and usually
about the facts - this time, too, and
for five centuries. But what isn't
known, in truth or fact, is what aspiring
novice raised his hand to humor
a disjunctive muse, to amuse himself,
and with or without intent to deceive,
deformed what Leonardo had begun.
Who was it conned the squint-eyed critics
who claim to know about these things:
what isn't seen, but what can be easily
imagined and created, that isn't there?

To avoid the edicts of past decrees,
today historians and connoisseurs
are cloistered in their studies consulting
their flagrant opinions, listing what they

have or haven't said or written about
"The Adoration," prepared to claim what
they suspected all along was not right.
Experts, like gods and artists, can be
easily enthroned, and adoration,
as the Magi knew, can paint
a century of fanciful, errant
stars on the thinnest air, any night.

In This House of Men

In This House of Men

Father

Failing biology he should not have been
a father after all, ill-suited as he was
during the depression years for anything
but looking for work to feed himself and
what little he could give to those who
depended on him. The clearer allusions
of human kindness were always unclear
in his mind. He was better left alone
in the dark workings of mechanical things
that tumbled in him machine-like
emitting primal responses from having
labored thirteen years as a farm hand
for immigrant parents who cast him out
at twenty-one, penniless. When at last
a patriarch he was no patriarch at all,
demanding both sustenance and care
from those he commanded. He should
not have attempted parenthood,
he should not have been a father after all.
He would have made a decent nomad or hobo.

Coach

Rock-ribbed, Republican, a withered leg,
an unyielding Puritan, he encouraged
others where he could not go. How often
do those without feet become cobblers?
Beneath the summer sun he required
little beyond an honest day's labor,

the seasoning with which work and work
will brand the soul. Knowing probability
and failure, he tallied each achievement
so in the evening shade success
was gauged not only in surviving
the day but in a dignity of what cunning
and strength had been crafted, what
competence earned by exploiting
natural gifts while weathering contradictions.
His nights were quiet and mostly
without light with which to find release
from the terrifying restrictions of nature.

Teacher
His beliefs were as apocryphal as his
teachings. The truth is that there is no
truth beyond a moment, beyond the facts
at hand, and believing does not make one
wise but otherwise. He said he could not
embrace human reason at its source - simply
enough, the journey was fraught with fallacies.
And so he chose a leap of faith,
from which to approach the dais,
which proved reason enough for him.
Then firm upon that shifting manifesto,
as tenuous as Socrates denying Crito's supplications,
he taunted the very gods he revered,
expecting them to stand their ground
in argument or deliver, with a flaming sword,

the salient insight that struck down Saul
meandering to Damascus. In order
to uphold the law Socrates committed suicide.
He should have died years before, but he did not.

Mystic
His connections rested in Platonic forms,
precarious and therefore often correct
wherein he blurred the demarcation
of the realms of sight and insight.
Real as they are, mirages will not slake
a traveler's thirst, though they may serve as an
indication of possibilities. For him
the soul was authentic enough to hold
in hand, to mold as a potter might mold
a vessel for fine wine. No flagellant -
fasting, corporeal punishment and pederasty
were as natural to him as a crown of thorns,
or any other failing of the flesh.
It's hell when everything substantial
is slightly out of focus, ephemeral as spirits
in your glass, the mountains obscured
by a morning mist. Women were to be
revered and eschewed, intuition the only way
to understanding, though it too was potted
with tar pits of deception and betrayal.

Brother

He might have been the Wandering Jew,
cursed by Christian epilogues lost
in the Diaspora of human failings,
or Diogenes with a lantern, disassociated
from family and friends in the noonday
sun looking not for an honest man
but for an authentic world - a man
constituted of the many parts of any
fragmented country where a desert
might be made fertile. A youth
in the wilderness, he gathered what
he could, arranging himself as an artist
might make a canvas of himself
with borrowed oils and stolen brushes.
Both cynic and renegade he made
alliances with myth, gave fraudulent
history a place in his home without
a homeland, and embraced, finally,
a remnant of humankind that was
neither gracious nor compassionate

When the State is Written Large

(May 3, 1960)

Even beyond the shadow of a doubt
for eleven women of the jury,
if Caryl Chessman was the Red Light Bandit

it would be iniquitous to take
his life for vengeance sake, or even just
for the hell of it. Whenever two

are gathered in the name of three, by what
authority do they judge? Absent
privy to their council, or lacking

an inclination for violence,
it is hard to tell. Those maligned by
failed lives and parents – enough to scar

the mind – live with things we'd all prefer
to not hold on to for too long. Is it
reasonable to kill the mind because

the body has gone wrong?
                              Among
the enclaves of his peers, certainly

Caryl Chessman was no favorite son.
But a decade in captivity,
of living day by day, someone

already with your end in mind, can turn
a man innocent, or at least within
Christian whimsy otherwise encourage

others to assume his guilt beyond
the intractability of act.
Here, what is done is done forever.

Though often bootless, we beg another
chance, fully expecting to have it.
Clemency, or even reprieves might

be as natural as the right to life.
Still, beneath the law, man conceives
a means to secret his conceits. Maybe

after all is spoken for and done,
the State is man written large, like holding
someone in a cage twelve years then

killing him.
               Waiting on a corner
for the light to change, the morning sky

an eternal blue, believing people can
forgive, I opened that day's news imagining
the thick black headlines would read,

"Chessman Spared!" and stepped into the street
numb enough nearly to forget how to walk.
Until a cabbie, or maybe a woman,

on her way to church with the kids,
leaned on the horn and yelled
                    "Watch out, you stupid shit!"

Hazlitt Spanking a Keswick Girl

Considering her esoteric and erratic past
she was fashionable enough to know better,
yet he certain she deserved the firmness
of his hand. For in the tangle of their trussed
and corseted alliance, pursuing her evasions,
he had given up any hope he might have had
of making her his own. So it was not the lifting
of her petticoats, but quite by accident
the unsnapping of a garter in the fray that
caused the sparks. But was it art?

His laying on of hands was not intended
to advance compliance, more a nurturing
enterprise by which she more than any
other might be brought to understand what
to expect from him. At any rate she took
offense, as she is wont to do, and raised
a hue and cry that nearly set the town alight
and led to the pursuit of errant William
across the countryside by that indignant
army that always occupies the night.

Yes, the garter made more of it than it was,
extending by implication his intentions, and
setting her to fear for what remained of her virtue.
In all likelihood until then she had been
entertained, maybe even pleased with him
enough to tolerate the guiding hand he lifted

in corrective playful abuse. But more than
the slap on her girdled rump the unsnapping
lit the fuse and the first dim glow of doubt
that she would have her way with him

crossed her mind. No longer a matter of ego,
the advantage in the balance, her fickle fashions
presaged in him a determination to have by other
means what he could not take by persuasion.
Clearly he had mistaken a siren for a muse,
and intent on having his bones she lifted her song,
as in her pleasant dance she often did her skirts,
encouraging that scourge of peasants who,
as no doubt William also had, were more than
willing to take her at her word, and in that
resolved to avenge his conceit by ducking him.

Here it was, his interest in her fair skin,
clothed or not, as well as whatever hope
he had of exacting retribution for her rebuke,
beat a quick retreat, as good companions
always will, over the hills to Dove Cottage.
That the pursuing entreaties did not emigrate
to London after him, showed the provinciality
of their composition, and how little effort
those so easily outraged are willing to expend
in defense of virtue and its random imaginings.

A Miracle of Two Tables

"I tried every 'excuse' to postpone putting the piece
of lead in its place. When, finally, with some reluctance
I was going to put it into its place, I said to myself:
'No! I do not want this piece of lead here; what I want
is a piece of paraffin.'"   Enrico Fermi

October 1938, Augustine's Rome,
the eternal streets infested with
ghost-like men, Enrico Fermi,

in his lab, with no intent to convert
the ruins to the City of God, one
afternoon contemplated his options.

Without hoping to alter the events
of humankind, or give alarm
to those making them, he turned

the ingot in his hands, regarding it
as if it might be Kryptonite.
Among the detritus of scrambled

signs and symbols he hesitated
between two tables, one of wood,
scar-crossed, a reject from another

lab, the second an age of sandstone
apart, though both, likened to the path
in Frost's yellow wood, needing wear.

In the heart of time and space itself,
he considered what he might not do
or undo next. Less capricious than

a buoyant Keats, who after reading
Chapman's Homer with a friend,
one pale night stared at the moon's

dull face and mistook Balboa
for Cortez, beneath the brilliant
Rosette light of day, Enrico pursuing

the alchemist's dream of transforming
nature's hidden and prudent ways,
stepped into the maze, now thought

to be without beginning that may
never end – the haze as dark and deadly
as any wood Dante might imagine.

It is not blinded men alone who are seared
by the Fates. To think him lost at that
crossroad would be to think too much.

As Adam strolled the paths of Eden
giving each thing its proper name,
Enrico entered the nether region

of that ancient thicket to discern and
label the perilous passages.
Con intuitio formidabile.

Knowing more than can be said, instead
of lead, he settled for paraffin,
and in a Cesium second dipped

his hand, and ours, into a bubbling
chaotic cauldron, a golden chalice,
setting on that ill-carved tablature,

on that shopworn altar of scarred-wood
a final fare of paradox and prophesy
fit for the condemned, be it god or man.

Mallory on Everest

Three-quarters of a century through
sun-soaked afternoons and Christmas nights
while women lighted candles in their rooms,
having descended that cross of stone,

reclining face-down, arms lifted heavenward
in an advanced repose of self-arrest
George Mallory clung to Everest.
The shards of broken rope, the frayed

ice-hardened harness of hemp and hope
girthed his loins in a nearly timeless
embrace (tethering him in place).
Scavenging Goraks picked away his flesh.

And the mountain, intent upon concealing
what it had done, covered his head
and shoulders with scree. The years of wind
and snow stripped away his coat and shirt

exposing his massive climber's lats,
the pearl-dull skin glowing in the white light
like a beacon sent out thousands of feet
above the chasm by one who again and again

seeks to pull himself into the clouds.
Of course the message is anything but clear.
Mountains are obdurate and dangerous
as are the conceits of men enthralled

by half with self-possession, another
half with a blinded disregard for schrunds,
their dedication absolute as any third-pole summit.
In part, as he said, "because it is there,"

Mallory tried to climb out of his skin.
But practiced and sanguine as they are,
seldom do climbers fashion ascents
as clean and straight as the fall-lines

gravity fastens to their feet. Over a deep,
coulior, on an out-cropping of mind
caught between thought and act, Mallory
lost his footing. No one can say if he

made the summit, or how, or even mark
a spot on the traverse where the wind caught
his heel. So there is no revelation here,
save the surest way to a dead-end –

to go up, then down. It took seventy-five
years to find him on a sun-thin afternoon,
at twenty thousand feet, and improvise
a grave to further compound the mystery.

Uncertainty may be more gracious than sinful.
Today Mallory rests without recompense
in his place on the rock-strewn slopes
beneath a fine white mist of blowing snow.

Slobodan Milosevec Poses to be Aged in Stone

Stand over there I tell him when he first appears,
facing the window, where the skylight empties out
onto the floor. Yes, that's it. If you will. Jedan

momennat, molim. Relax, assume a proper posture,
confident, so to speak, and think about becoming stone.
Now, lift your chin a bit. Set your eyes on the Sava,

and I will set them in your head as clear and hard
as Augustus of Prima Porta. Please, do not raise
your hands. Remain calm. Keep them at your sides,

with slight anticipation, as if you are about to touch
something you have never touched before. Remember
who you are, so it will be reflected in your face. Yes,

put your trust in stone. Become stone as the stone
becomes you. Know you have chosen well coming
here, as I have chosen basalt to befit the Balkans

and satisfy the Ministry of Antiquity and Museums.
Basalt has such exquisite qualities of space and time.
It is more attractive than marble, clings to form,

resists disfigurement. And oh, the subtle insinuations
it can offer light. This piece, not perfect, mind you,
but worthy as any I have found, possessed of contours

I will liberate, made practical and, therefore, more
desirable by its flaws. If all the world is just a bit
of time, let this be yours. What we do here will deny

violent storms, outlive whole peoples. A thousand
years from now patrons will polish your countenance
with their scarves. You'll be revered far more then

than you are today. Do not be impatient. Gaze out
the window to the tree lined streets, the National Theater,
Knez Milos astride his horse. It is impossible to know

how long this will take. Today I'll make a few quick
sketches, then, imate vezu. Turn now, one angle, another
in a week or so. Chiaroscuro, da Vinci called it. And

though I am not Leonardo, it will serve us well. Vasa
molba ce biti odobrena. I'll apply the same sure hands
my father gave his years of blinded faith to the transept

of Saint Sophia's. You see, he was a stonecutter,
his violent art tempered only by imperiled belief,
and beneath the hammer, day by day, in small ways,

you too, will become the curve and cut of stone. I'll give
you what the people want, and in that give them you.
As they say, ars est calare artum - my task to find

something of beauty in what remains so grievously
unfinished in nature. Veluti in speculum, a valid adage,
I'm sure you can appreciate, to fit what you most desire.

The mudded boots and tattered uniform, stained fingers,
the coat, for affect, a size too large, threadbare and
shabby with malignance and excess. The slack mouth,

enfeebled jaw, yes, and the thickened brow of myopic
yearning. All of these. Velika je steta. I'll liberate you
from the stone. I'll set you free - as it becomes you.

Jedan momenat, moirn - One moment, please.
Imate vezu - You are through.
Vasa molba ce biti odobrenda - Your request will he granted.
Ars est calare artum - Art covets up art.
Veluti in speculum - Reflected as in a mirror.
Velikaje steta - It is a great pity.

Pontiac in Cahokia

It isn't clear what he was doing in the store that day.
He may have hoped to trade, and finding nothing,

no English Devil to dicker with, entertained himself,
sipping a cup of whiskey dipped from the open barrel

at the door. He had navigated the not too subtle river
currents that morning, crossing from Laclede's mansion,

the bear and raven on the prow of his canoe pushed
quietly into turbulent waters. His chiseled profile,

his warrior-cropped hair, made famous by Detroit
and the British dead, set against the great north, the red

of his coat, the golden epaulettes glowing in the sun,
he chanted an aubade for the day, those incantations

of human voice meant to beguile. All of him smelled
of the bear grease he rubbed on to keep away the cold.

Speaking with the clerk in broken French he moved
around the store, examined merchandise, shadowed

by Black Dog's silent nephew. There were axes, knives,
lacquered rifle stocks. He turned them over carefully,

caressing the hard wood with the flat of his hand,
holding each up to balance, testing the weight to his grip

with a chief's appreciation, as if it were something
he might use for another purpose. And blankets,

machine made by now, from the east. Maybe he had
in mind the women at the mouth of the Maumee

working evenings by firelight. He didn't buy anything.
He might have come among the Illinois that morning

just for the hell of it, to be seen, to spook the English,
to annoy the locals, to fuel rumors of a new and again

dangerous federation. Maybe his warriors' memory
had forgotten the blood he spilled, the dead. Finding

nothing of interest in the store, he hung the empty cup
at the rim of the barrel. He knew harm finds only those

who encourage it, believing, as warriors do, that there
is no bullet meant for him. He had done what any

capable man would have done. The British and French
could not harm him. Going out he offered a small prayer

to the sun. He directed, then permitted the youthful
Peoria brave to step aside as he passed, to bludgeon him

from behind. He slipped to his knees, the soft syllables
of the chant to keep him from harm, his voice weak

and nearly gone by then, allowing Black Dog's nephew
to do what the gods and the British had failed to do,
                    to sink a knife deep in his chest.

Shreve Steps Out of the Haufbrau
To Look at the Sky

For the Paul Shreve Memorial
at the Haufbrau, Bozeman, Montana
February 13, 2010

He was here just a minute ago
sitting over there in that chair,
the spindle-backed affair with

his name carved on it. The pack
of Camels on the table, the one
in the ashtray glowing like a star

on a bad winter night, the Bic lighter,
the worn pencil, the empty
shot glass, are his. A Norther

was pushing at the window
and he stepped out to investigate,
to check on what might be tracking

in from the mountains. The weather
moves in and out of our lives.
Nobody wants to get caught

in a blizzard. People show up
with wind and frost in their hair
and just that quickly they disappear.

If you look closely you'll see
his hat and coat are still there
on the chair, his finger prints

on the table. If you listen you might
hear his harp blowin' the blues
on the juke-box, maybe even feel

his warm impression on the air.
That will last the longest – hanging
in the smoke, in the soft haze and

hum of voices, an imprint, a pliant
memory on the dim room. Departures
like beginnings are illusory. Just

when you think someone is gone,
they reappear. So don't move
anything. Save his place at the table.

But like I say, keep a sharp eye
on the door. He'll come in from
the parking lot one of these days

to wait for the wind to die down,
the snow to clear and a small sun
to shine on the back roads of Fence-line

poems, to wait until there's goodwill
enough for the soul to gather up energy
and take on a human form again,

to shape an old body with new life –
enough material for another run
of Want-ad stories. Leave his chair

there – his hat, his coat, the shot-glass,
the cigarette with the long ash, and
the pencil stub. Let's just leave it there.